THEODORE GERICAULT

(1791-1824)

W9-BWW-231

Acknowledgments

We would like to thank the following individuals and institutions whose generous assistance has made possible the quality and scope of this exhibition:

Elita and William Agee; Richard Burton, Sylvie Skira and Jerry Crompton of BCK Graphic Arts; Jean-Luc Bordeaux; Mark Brady; Robert Buck, Director, Linda Ferber, Chief Curator, Sarah Faunce, Chairman of Painting and Sculpture, The Brooklyn Museum; Sheldon Clark; Karen and Arthur Cohen; Madame Dubaut; Annette and Robert Elowitch, Barridoff Galleries; Neal Fiertag; Marco Grassi; Dr. Paul Joannides, Oxford; Dr. Lee Johnson; Annette and Myron Kaplan; Mrs. Eva Kreis of the Swiss Institute for Art Research; Mr. and Mrs. Jan Krugier, Diane Upright and James Baron; Helen and Daniel Lindsay; Gilda and Thomas LiPuma; John Maroulis; Liz Martin, Stanford University; Katherine Baetjer, Curator of European Paintings, Jacob Bean, Curator of Drawings, Everett Fahy, Chairman of European Paintings, Gary Tinterow, Curator of European Paintings, The Metropolitan Museum of Art; George Keyes, Curator of Paintings, Alan Shestack, Director; The Minneapolis Institute of Art; Hans Meyer; Vera Meyer; Erika Billeter, Director, Musée Cantonal des Beaux-Arts; Marc Wilson, Director, George McKenna, Curator of Prints and Drawings, Nelson-Atkins Museum of Art; Jill Newhouse; G. Nimberger; Simon Parkes; Willem deLooper, Director, Joseph Holbach, Registrar, The Phillips Collection; Alex Raydon; Irwin Rosen, Hudson Shipping Co.; Alan Salz; Kate Schaeffer; Dr. Max Schmidheiny; Stanford University Museum of Art; David Brooke, Director, Alexandra Murphy, Associate Curator, Martha Asher, Registrar, Sterling and Francine Clark Art Institute; Jean-Marc Tassel; Betsy Rosasco, Associate Curator, Allen Rosenbaum, Director, The Art Museum, Princeton University; Frank Trapp; Eugene V. Thaw and Patricia Tang; Bernadette d'Ussel, Jet Art Shipping; Paul Perrot, Director, Pinkney Near, Chief Curator, Virginia Museum of Fine Arts; Margit and Rolf Weinberg; Wheelock Whitney; Dominic Tambini and Harry Brooks, Wildenstein and Co.; Dr. Mary Neill, Director, Michael Komanecky, Assistant to the Director, Yale University Art Gallery.

We would like to give special thanks to the following individuals whose cooperation, assistance and knowledge was invaluable to this project: Dr. Lorenz Eitner, Stanford University; Philippe Grunchec, Director, Musée des Beaux-Arts, Paris; Dr. Hans Lüthy, Swiss Institute for Art Research; and Dr. Peter Nathan, Galerie Nathan, Zurich.

Finally, thanks to: Nanci Barbal, Lori B. Bookstein, Ronald Gersten, Joan LiPuma, Megan Moynihan and Randall P. Soucy for their efforts on behalf of this project. Particular mention to Heather B. Nevin for her work on the production of this catalogue and exhibition.

© 1987 Salander-O'Reilly Galleries Inc.
Photography: Sylvia Sarner, N.Y.
Library of Congress No. 87 — 60891

THEODORE GERICAULT
(1791-1824)

An exhibition
Paintings, Drawings, Watercolors,
Prints and Sculpture

ESSAYS
DR. LORENZ EITNER
OSGOOD HOOKER PROFESSOR OF FINE ARTS
STANFORD UNIVERSITY
CHAIRMAN, ART DEPARTMENT
DIRECTOR, STANFORD MUSEUM

DR. HANS LÜTHY
SWISS INSTITUTE FOR ART RESEARCH,
ZURICH
DIRECTOR

Salander-O'Reilly Galleries, Inc.
22 East 80 Street New York, NY 10021, Tel. 212 879-6606

Marine
Marine (c. 1822-23)
oil on canvas 18½ × 22¹/₁₆
Catalogue no. 26

INTRODUCTION

By Lorenz Eitner

The dispersal of Gericault's work after his death, and the subsequent efforts of collectors and scholars to reconstitute it, recall the myth of Osiris whose dismembered body, its fragments scattered throughout Egypt, was piously reassembled by Isis. Gericault has become a momentous presence in the landscape of modern art, but it cannot yet be said that we see him whole: the work of Isis is still in progress, hindered not only by the disappearance of some important pieces, but also by the difficulty of separating the authentic remains from an accretion of false attributions and of replacing them in their proper order.

When Gericault died, at the age of thirty-three, he was known to the public by only three paintings that had been exhibited at the Salon, the *Charging Chasseur* (1812), the *Wounded Cuirassier* (1814), and the *Raft of the Medusa* (1819), and by a handful of lithographs. The sale of his studio, in 1824, abruptly dispersed some 220 paintings and sixteen large lots of drawings and watercolors that included a number of sketchbooks, subsequently disassembled, and may have comprised as many as 1,600 to 1,800 individual sheets. Save for some gifts to friends and relatives, this constituted the bulk of his life's work. He had sold very little.

External circumstances and the complexities of his own nature contributed to the seemingly inconclusive, experimental variety and stylistic inconsistency of his legacy, which abounds in daring ideas, abortive projects, and restless probings, but contains few fully realized works. His life took its brief course (1791-1824) against a background of catastrophic change and upheaval. Gericault came into the world in the midst of the Revolution; he experienced the exaltation of Napoleon's triumphs in his boyhood, reached maturity during the Empire's decline, and ended his career of little more than twelve working years in the troubled early part of the Restoration. Born to a new-rich family of the provincial middle-class, remote from artistic or intellectual interests, he startled his relatives by his decision, at age seventeen, to become a painter. His early training, casual and seemingly without direction, foreshadowed the dilemmas that he was to face in his later career. He first sought guidance from Carle Vernet, a facile modernist and elegant horse painter, but soon left this genial, light-hearted mentor for Pierre Guérin, a rigorous classicist and conscientious teacher. Gericault proved to be a difficult pupil who persevered in his attendance at Guérin's studio for only about a year. Neoclassicism by that time had begun to harden into routines too lifeless for an artist of Gericault's ardent temperament. Guérin recognized the talent of his unruly disciple, but disapproved of his impulsive variability, and warned his other, more docile students against imitating this undisciplined youth who, unlike them, possessed "the stuff of three or four painters".

Gericault soon left his master to study on his own at the Louvre, recently transformed into the Musée Napoleon and filled with the loot of the Flemish and Italian campaigns. Here he set up his easel before paintings by Rubens, Rembrandt, Velasquez, and Titian in which he discovered a richness and vitality that eclipsed the reasoned compositions of the Davidian school. He persisted in his copying of the masters for about six years, from 1810 until 1815, a remarkably sustained effort, compared to the brevity of his studies with Vernet and Guérin. Like most of the leading painters of his century, he must be reckoned as an essentially self-trained artist, whose school was the museum, who chose his teachers from the masters of the past, and who, guided by instinctive sympathies, gradually defined his artistic personality by his choice of models. The examples of his copies of the masters included in the present exhibition indicate the breadth of his interest and prove that copying, far from stifling his individuality, gave him the courage to indulge a very personal love of heavy pigment and sensuous brushwork.

His first major independent work bore the mark of his museum studies. The large canvas of the *Charging Chasseur* that caused a stir at the Salon of 1812 was a bold improvisation on a contemporary theme, but one that reflected his knowledge of the old masters. The image of an officer of the Imperial Guards rushing into battle on his wildly rearing horse had a pointed, quasi-emblematical significance in the year of Napoleon's assault on Russia. The picture's style was indebted to the dynamic colorism of Gros, the modern master whom Gericault particularly admired, but it ultimately derived from Baroque sources—beyond its immediate, modern models, it pointed to Rubens.

The years that followed this precocious success—Gericault was twenty-one years old in 1812—were troubled and, on the surface, unproductive. He continued his self-training, copied at the Louvre, and painted the posing nude in Guérin's studio. Renouncing the ambitious monumentality and dramatics of the *Chasseur* for the time being, he devoted himself to work of small scale and minutely delicate execution. The studies of horses and the portraits of Napoleonic cavalrymen that he painted in 1812-14 have a lively freshness of color and deftness of handling that suggest a change of direction. They mark the first of the recurrent episodes of stylistic relaxation that were regularly to follow Gericault's more strenuous efforts, a temporary subsidence into a casual, descriptive realism that came easily to him. But such undemanding work did not satisfy him for long. He began to search for a more powerful and emotionally affecting style, perhaps in response to the Empire's disastrous fall.

At the Salon of 1814, held not long after Napoleon's abdication, he exhibited his somber *Wounded Cuirassier,* a mournful pendant to the victorious *Chasseur* of 1812. The ponderous figure of the defeated soldier, sculpturally compact in its metal armor and earth-bound weight, lacked the painterly brilliance and dashing modernity of the earlier picture. It seemed not only a more labored, but also a less progressive work. Gericault himself was dissatisfied. The *Cuirassier,* nonetheless, marked an advance on his way toward an art of monumental format and energetic expression. It was accompanied by other military portraits, of similar style and mood, though of smaller format and private purpose. The *Mounted Hussar Trumpeter* of the Williamstown Clark Art Institute, included in this exhibition, typifies these evocations of military valor in defeat. The massive figures in them are seen from a vantage point so low as to make them loom, like monuments, against their backgrounds. In their melancholy stillness and

gravity, they present a striking contrast to the liveliness of Gericault's brilliant equestrians of the time of the *Charging Chasseur.*

Gericault had hoped, somewhat naively, that his Salon entries might be purchased by the Government. The *Chasseur* received a gold medal in 1812, the *Wounded Cuirassier* was rated a failure in 1814, and both pictures remained on Gericault's hands, to his intense disappointment. His attempt to win recognition, in competition with the more conventionally trained artists of his generation, had miscarried. He continued to be thought of by his friends, and perhaps by himself, as a gentleman-painter. A legacy which his mother had left him allowed him to live in comfort, without having to sell his work. This gave him the freedom to experiment at his pleasure, but it also removed the spur of necessity without which he found it difficult to concentrate on one goal and to carry his work to completion. What nevertheless compelled him to persevere, despite periods of lassitude and discouragement, was an intense ambition to distinguish himself by work of the grandest scale and power. There was in him an urge "to shine, to illuminate, to astonish the world," a declamatory strain, an impulse to exaggeration that went far beyond his natural facility and his gift for intimate realism. He recognized the limitations of his talent and the incompleteness of his education, and resolved to make a new start, even at the risk of destroying something in himself.

Some time in early 1815, he rather abruptly abandoned the modern, national subjects with which he had identified himself for the past three years and embarked on a rigorous course of self-training in an effort to acquire a new style. The reasons for this break were complex. With the disappearance of Napoleon, modern history painting had lost its patron and its inspiration, and become a private genre. Artists who, like Gericault, had the ambition of working on a monumental scale faced a dilemma: they had to make a choice between modernity and monumentality, giving up one or the other—or attempt to discover a new form of modern history painting. Upsets in his private life, an unfortunate, brief enlistment in a royal cavalry regiment, and the beginning of a clandestine love affair, may have contributed to his need for a change. For nearly two years he inflicted on himself all the rigors of the kind of academic regimen that he had once refused to accept from his master, Pierre Guérin. He rehearsed the rudiments of figure construction and composition, taking his motifs from the repertory of classicist stock types that he had shunned in his student days. By inborn talent a colorist and realist, he deliberately thwarted his spontaneous inclinations, replaced color with sharp light-dark contrasts, painterly effect with contour design, and in his treatment of the human figure limited himself to a vocabulary of rough stereotypes, emphatically heavy and angular, harsh to the point of crudity, and entirely indifferent to natural appearance.

The style that Gericault distilled from this self-inflicted ordeal has little to do with conventional classicism, though he used it to express classical themes, the loves of the gods and the battles of giants. He seized on the faded clichés of neoclassicism with a kind of fury, combining something of Flaxman's abstraction with a touch of Guérin's melodrama in rough-hewn compositions of extraordinary vigor. His very personal intent was to gain greater expressive force: more important than the increase in control was the increase in energy that discipline had brought him. Unlike his earlier, casual realism, this new, highly artificial manner lent itself to resonant statements. Romantic in its intensity, borrowed from the tradition of Michelangelo rather than that of David, it extended his range to include fantasies of terror, cruelty, and lust.

The dramatic energy that informs these compositional exercises also appears in some of Gericault's paintings of this period and in a few sculptural essays. There can be no doubt that the main purpose of these efforts was to prepare himself for painting on a monumental scale. For the time being, he applied his grand style to work of modest scale, at times with rather strange results. Thus he gave an oddly Michelangelesque flavor to the *Portrait of Alfred Dedreux* (Metropolitan Museum), the five-year-old son of a friend. More appropriately, he used it in the series of studies of heroic male nudes which he appears to have painted by way of rehearsal for the Rome Prize competition of 1816, in which he participated in the hope of winning a stipend for the Villa Medici. He failed the second round of the contest, precisely that of the study of the posing model, and was thus disqualified from competing in the final, decisive trial.

Despite this setback, Gericault was determined to go to Rome, partly to further his self-education, partly to escape the torments of an unavowable love affair. In Florence and Rome, he was overwhelmed by the works of Michelangelo, he "trembled before the masters of Italy, doubted his own ability, and only gradually recovered from this shock." His newly-acquired style had by now lost much of its initial harshness, and his irrepressible virtuosity was beginning to reassert itself, despite the obstacles he had put in its way. With superb assurance, he drew a succession of erotic fantasies on classical themes—Centaurs abducting Nymphs, Silenus in procession, Leda in the swan's embrace. The fear that he might lapse into elegant routine prompted him to seek new problems. Mythological subjects did not deeply interest him. After his long ordeal of stylistic discipline, he felt the need for fresh experience. Equally impressed by the drama of Italian life and the greatness of Italian art, he conceived the idea of treating an observation gathered in the streets of modern Rome in an elevated style reminiscent of Michelangelo or Raphael. An event of the Roman carnival of 1817, the traditional race of the riderless Barberi horses in the Corso, gave him the motif he needed. He began by recording the start of the race as he had actually seen it in the Piazza del Popolo, a turbulent and diffuse crowd scene. In a series of studies, he then gradually reduced the panoramic modern spectacle to a few, clearly articulated groups, arranged these in a balanced frieze, stripped the figures of their modern costumes, and transformed the piazza into a colonnaded forum suggestive of ancient rather than modern Rome. The final preparatory design of the *Race of the Barberi Horses,* ready to be transferred to a large canvas, projected a severely stylized composition of athletes struggling with horses, in a setting of undefined location and a time neither ancient nor modern. Had Gericault executed it in the vast dimensions which he envisaged, he would have produced a work entirely without parallel in its time: a painting of heroic format and grand style, without definable subject; a self-sufficient image, impressive in its formal dignity, suggestive of high significance, but withholding all clues to the nature of the event or situation represented, and giving no hint of any connection with history, literature, or simple reality. Having conceived this feat of thematic abstraction, he stopped short of carrying it out. He had never before taken a project so far—the *Chasseur* and *Cuirassier* by comparison had been rapid improvisations—and in the end, perhaps remembering his earlier disappointments at the Salon, lost the courage and energy necessary for its final execution. Far sooner than he had planned, he left Rome and returned to France.

Back in Paris, he briefly continued his experimentation with timeless, heroic subjects, composing a *Cattle Market,* another contest between men and beasts, and a *Battle Scene* which he alternately cast in an antique and a modern version. The scattered remnants of theser projects are among the most impressive examples of his grand manner. But in the rush of Paris, the solemn visions soon faded, too remote to compete with the vivid reality that surrounded Gericault on all sides. His personal life was approching a crisis. He had resumed his love affair with a close relative, the young wife of an elderly uncle who was at the head of the family firm. In the late fall of 1817, his mistress conceived a child by him. The fear of the impending, inevitable scandal prompted him to seek refuge in work, but the ideas that had occupied him in his Italian solitude now seemed to him to lack interest. He had come to a dead end, and the thought of the approaching Salon must have filled him with anxiety. Four years had passed since he had last exhibited a painting. His long effort of self-training had as yet produced nothing of importance. Forgotten by the public, and pitied by his friends who believed that he had squandered his talent, Gericault was determined to change this situation by making a spectacular appearance at the forthcoming Salon of 1819. Turning his Italian experience to new advantage, he conceived of the idea of representing exemplary acts of courage or endurance, taken from recent modern history, with the formality and elevation of style with which he had treated themes from classical mythology.

While waiting for the right subject to come his way, he followed the news of the day and tried his hand at work of small format and wholly modern character. The new medium of lithography, very recently introduced to France and used mainly for journalistic or illustrative work, offered him a chance to try out contemporary subjects. In the military scenes which he drew on the stone in 1818, he found a way of reconciling realistic observation with stylistic discipline, and achieved on a small scale that union of the grand and the natural which he hoped to realize in the much more ambitious format of his projected Salon painting. He appears to have thought for a moment that he had found his subject in accounts of a recent, atrocious crime, the murder of Fualdes, a former magistrate of Rodez, which he proposed to represent in the "antique style".

The crowning result of these various efforts was the *Raft of the Medusa* with which Gericault did create a sensation at the Salon of 1819. The huge canvas represents the aftermath of a shipwreck which, three years earlier, had violently aroused public opinion in France. Gericault was initially attracted to the subject by its sensational actuality and controversiality, but in the course of giving it pictorial form it gradually progressed from reportorial realism to a philosophical statement—from an indictment of a corrupt naval establishment to a dramatization of mankind's struggle against the destructive power of nature. The problem he set himself was an extremely difficult one: he wanted to achieve a synthesis of the two contrary tendencies in his work, by treating an actual, modern occurrence in the exalted language of monumental art. The newspaper story of the wreck of a government frigate and subsequent abandonment of part of its crew was to be raised to the tragic power of Michelangelo's *Last Judgement* or Dante's *Inferno.*

He went about his task with his accustomed thoroughness, as the large number of preparatory studies shows. Before settling his composition, he systematically explored the successive episodes of the underlying narrative: the outbreak of mutiny and of cannibalism of the raft; the victims' first inconclusive sighting of the distant rescue vessel on the thirteenth day of their ordeal; and the final rescue of the few survivors. In the end, he chose the moment of the highest suspense between hope and dispair,when the rescue vessel briefly appeared to the shipwrecked on the raft, because it offered the strongest pictorial effect and expressed the particular significance he wished to give the event. Once he had found his subject, he very gradually constructed its compositional form in a long series of contour drawings, after which he translated it, in several oil studies, into the painterly terms of light and color. For the execution of the large, final canvas, he posed studio models in the positions called for by the compositional design, and painted all the figurers and faces directly from the life, literally fleshing out the imagined scene with the substance of observed reality.

Masterfully composed in such a way as to force the viewer into a close involvement with its action, the image delivers its meaning, without any narrative devices, by its very structure. But it cannot be said that it entirely fulfils Gericault's aim of reconciling realism and grand style. In the *Raft of the Medusa's* final form, the calculated composition and the strenuous gigantism of the figures clash with the realism of the execution. Despite the beauty of many of its parts, the *Raft* attains neither the stylistic unity of Gericault's purely idea compositions, nor the troubling reality of his studies from the life.

At the Salon, the picture met with a mixed reception. The public, fascinated by its subject matter, paid it much attention; the critics blamed or praised it for reasons that had much to do with its political implications, and very little with its artistic quality. Disappointed and nervously exhausted after what had been the longest and most strenuous exertion of his career he renounced the grand manner and declared his intention of "returning to the stables," i.e. to the less demanding forms of realism. He went to England to exhibit his picture to the paying public, and here renewed acquaintance with those essentially anticlassical traditions of genre and portraiture to which Carle Vernet had first introduced him more than a decade earlier. As his interest in heroic monumentality waned, the other side of his talent, the innate gift for intimate realism and sensuous color, came to the fore again, seconded by his impressions of English art. With a new lightness of touch, he drew or painted in watercolor horsemen, farriers, waggoners, beggars, and the animals at the zoological garden. His manner lost much of its former hard energy, and instead stressed subtleties of texture, tone, and color. It was a time of exploration during which he showed himself to be nervously receptive to new impressions. Struck by the spectacle of urban poverty, he drew studies of the poor whom he observed in the streets of London, and used some of these for a series of lithographs, published in London in 1821, which deal with social reality without moralizing or sentimentality. The somber

objectivity with which they describe suffering and human decay in their actual urban settings had no close parallel in French or English art of the period. Others of his English works are concerned, by contrast, with elegant horsemanship and sport, most notably the only large, highly finished painting of his English period, the *Epsom Downs Derby,* the modern, English counterpart to his classical Roman Race of the Barberi Horses.

When he returned to Paris, at the end of 1821, his health had begun to fail. His life was now rapidly winding down to its end. Frequently ill, he suffered from what seemed to his friends a kind of physical and moral fatigue. An urge to self-destruction, barely concealed, seemed to guide his conduct in these last years. The repeated riding accidents, which succeeded in breaking what remained of his health, the ruinous speculations and reckless expenditures that brought him to the edge of want, and the reported attempts at suicide give the impression of a purpose followed, a death wish rapidly carried out. His artistic powers were unimpaired, but instead of focusing them on major projects, he now spent them on a multitude of enterprises of small ambition and short duration. He had lived most of his life comfortably on his inheritance, able to work as he pleased, without giving a thought to the salability of his work. The loss of a large part of his fortune in 1822 compelled him to begin working for the market and to suit himself to the tastes of collectors and dealers. This accounts for his large production, in 1822-23, of highly finished watercolors and small oil paintings of pleasing subjects, horse genres for the most part, romantic exotica, and illustrations of popular, mainly Byronic literature.

The few salient works that rise above this level of refined but minor accomplishment all had some private significance, and evidently drew on deeper resources of emotional energy. The great achievement of his last years was not to be another grand Salon picture, but a series of portraits of ten insane men and women, the patients of a medical friend, Dr. E. J. Georget, a pioneer of psychiatric medicine, who may have asked Gericault to paint them as a record of his clinical research. The five surviving portraits of the series repesent victims of various delusions, or "monomanias". Gericault painted them with severe objectivity, in a format that leaves no doubt about their purely private purpose. The sharply illuminated faces of the sufferers emerge with hypnotic insistence from the shadowy backgrounds. In their profound realism, free of romantic sentiment or artistic dramatization, they mark Gericault's final achievement—a form of painting at once true to reality and powerfully expressive, without resort to stylistic artifice. They define his place in the European vanguard as distinctly as the *Raft of the Medusa,* yet remained unknown for a century, and were among the last of his works to reach a wider public.

In the spring of 1823, Gericault's fatal illness, tubercular in origin, became acute. He realized that he was dying, and bitterly regretted his many unfinished projects, his frequent changes of direction, and the waste of his talent on petty enterprises. As he lay on his sick bed, his old ambition to paint subjects from modern life on a hugely monumental scale returned with full force. Too weak for their actual execution, he busied himself with the preliminaries for several large compositions, including the *Opening of the Doors of the Spanish Inquisition* and the *African Slave Trade,* subjects of intense political interest to liberal Frenchmen of the period. Coming after several years of small-scale work, these last projects amount to a final gesture in the direction of great subjects and grand style. Though realized only in the form of drawings, their conception equals that of the *Raft of the Medusa* in ambition and surpasses it in stylistic unity. Had he lived longer, they might have competed at the Salon with Delacroix' *Massacres at Scio* and *Liberty on the Barricade.* But Gericault died, in January of 1824, at the age of thirty-three.

His work remained a fragment, yet its widely scattered parts can be seen to form a pattern of remarkable symmetry. The various strands of his talent, disjoined at the beginning, gradually converged and came to a focus in the *Raft of the Medusa* in his mid-career, only to diverge again into various directions during his later years, though with some promise—tragically unfulfilled—of an ultimate, more complete union.

Stanford University, March 1987.

THE TEMPERAMENT OF GERICAULT

FOR MAX SCHMIDHEINY

BY HANS A. LÜTHY

During his relatively short career, Gericault led a life that would have filled several normal artists' lives. His decision in 1812 to paint the *Charging Chasseur* and to submit the large canvas to the jury of the Salon was a daring, albeit successful, venture. Even the similarily precocious Delacroix entered the Salon comparatively three years later than Gericault. The often-quoted exclamation by David, "D'où cela sort-il? Je ne reconnais pas cette touche,"[1] shows the surprise of a "chef d'école", who was accustomed to recognizing the new-comers in the sacred halls of the Salon; these leading artists followed the careers of the more talented students in ateliers other than their own.

This essay tries to link the character of Gericault with certain aspects of his artistic work, primarily with the lesser known drawings, which up until now, have not been dealt with in a larger context. These drawings are mainly from the period between 1815 and 1817, corresponding to the time before and during his stay in Italy. However, we first have to recall the events following the still limited success of the *Chasseur* of 1812. Our knowledge of Gericault's life in 1813 and 1814 is very limited. The young painter exhibited three paintings at the Salon of 1814: again the *Chasseur,* a presently lost scene entitled *Exercice à feu dans la plaine de Grenelle* and the *Wounded Cuirassier.* Near the end of the year, Gericault joined the Gray Muskateers, and then accompanied, in March 1815, the King of France to Belgium. This incident seems to be more relevant than a simple military adventure. In light of Gericault's Napoleonic ideals after 1817, this royalist engagement turned out to be ephemeral and hasty. Lorenz Eitner believes Gericault was much more attracted by the horses of the royal troupe and the military glitter than by the impact of a political conviction.[2]

Around the same time, perhaps connected with the military involvement, Gericault fell in love with his aunt Alexandrine-Modeste Caruel, six years older than her now twenty-four year old nephew. The affair, only known in detail since the

publication of related documents in 1976 by the archivist Michel Le Pesant,[3] deeply determined Gericault's life until his death. His trip to Italy from October 1816 to October 1817 was also a flight from the ill-fated relationship with Alexandrine-Modeste. Charles Clément, the most reliable source for the artist's life and cataloguer of his work in the Nineteenth century, knew the story but withheld his knowledge because of its implications for the living members of the families Caruel and Gericault. In a very discreet manner Clément passed over these months: "Une affectation partagée, irrégulière, orageuse, et qu'il ne pouvait avouer, où il avait apporté toute la violence de son caractère et de son tempérament... le troublait jusqu'au fond."[4]

During this one and a half years between the engagement in the Muskateers and the departure to Italy, a new and spectacular group of drawings must be connected with Gericault's private life.[5] The iconography of these drawings covers an area of violent action between human beings, including rape, slaughter, murder and torture, but also less violent motifs of "Satyr and Nymph". Prior to the years 1815-16, Gericault limited action in his art to military scenes, such as single charging officers or battles, which were at this time very popular subjects. The eruption of this new iconography shows no parallels in contemporary French art; only Goya, and some decades earlier, Fuseli, created similar works.

One of the difficulties in dealing with the group is the titles of the drawings. Even Charles Clément had problems in cataloging Gericault's drawings.[6] The related motifs are scattered throughout the chronologically arranged catalogue and bear such titles as "Croquis divers" (Clément no. 79), "Démons" (Clément no. 105) or "La Rixe" (Clément no. 166). Even for Clément, it was difficult to understand how Gericault could do a drawing without describing a traditional subject. For Gericault to follow his own thoughts or dreams in creating such fantastic motifs, was outside the normal artistic rules. We may assume that the emotionally troubled love affair infected the already shaken character of the artist and opened the door for new orbits in artistic creation.

The work in question may be divided chronologically into two groups, one formed in 1815-16 in Paris, and the other in 1816-17 in Italy. The earlier cluster contains about twenty sheets, today in different museums and private collections. Stylistically, they correspond to a return to classicism, but in a very different way than contemporary academism. Lorenz Eitner characterized this change as an "explosion of energy, like that produced by a flow of lava on a bed of ice."[7] Part of the drawings in context may still be connected with classical themes; one cluster of drawings revolves around the subject of "Centaurs carrying off women",[8] another depicts "Leda and the Swan".[9] A third group comprises those with no decipherable titles, showing coupled men and women fighting and torturing each other. The several known drawings of satyrs and nymphs,[10] linked with the original sculpture *Satyr and Nymph* (Rouen, Musée), by comparison, lack the original power of the untitled groups.

Lorenz Eitner dates the Centaur and Leda drawings to the years 1816-17, and sees them as a sublimation of the "earlier, darker fantasies."[11] There is, in fact, not only an iconographical change, but also a different control of pen and pencil; the earlier drawings show thick contours and strong contrasts in light and shadow. The second group has lost the more sculptural effect for a more painterly handling of the outlines and plasticity of the body-volumes. The mythologically defined works, however, are based essentially on the earlier ones, and their mastery would not have been possible without the previous experience.

Prior to 1815, as said previously, Gericault did not depict much action. During his stay in Rome and until 1820, action and violence seem temporarily to dominate his artistic work. The *Race of the Barberi Horses* and the *Cattle Market*, both conceived in Italy, demonstrate human beings and animals in full movement, often fighting one another. Gericault's first project for the 1819 Salon illustrated the case of the murdered businessman Fualdès, which was a cloak-and-dagger story he exploited in several pictorial drawings. The *Raft of the Medusa* itself presents many occasions for outspoken frenzy, and Gericault, in the development of his final composition, went through nearly all the tumultuous episodes and adventures on the raft. With the iconographical and compositional work of the *Raft,* Gericault seems to have exhausted this field and neither his lithographs nor the themes from England show aspects of vehement action.

The personalization of iconography at the beginning of the Nineteenth century is exceptional. One could object that Gericault made the drawings in 1815-16 only for his private pleasure, and would be correct, but the main issue lies elsewhere and seems to be hidden in the extraordinary character of the artist. In examining the few personal reports of Gericault's life, we get the impression of a fierce and easily aroused temper. His relationship with horses and wild rides, leading finally to his early death, is all too well known to be discussed here. Among the most typical traits of his character were his mood changes; from the deepest depression to exuberant high spirits. The letter of Th. Lebrun to Feuillet de Conches[12] tells of a not-so-funny story about a visit by Lebrun to Gericault's apartment. Gericault had put curlers in his hair, and as Lebrun told him about cancelling their joint travel to Italy, Gericault believed his uncommon appearance to be the reason for the change. Lebrun could only convince him of the futility of the argument with the greatest of difficulty. Another example is given by Gericault's close friend Charlet: Gericault tried one evening to kill himself in an English hotel, but was saved by Charlet. After a short discussion Gericault burst into laughter and promised Charlet not to repeat the attempt.[13]

*

*   *

Gericault's relationship with the opposite sex still holds mystery. The affair with Alexandrine-Modeste continued after Gericault's return to Italy and caused further havoc. I refer here to the biography by Lorenz Eitner and his excellent description of the clandestine and tragic love. With the birth of a son in August 1818, Alexandrine-Modeste was forced to abandon her family, and we know nothing of further meetings. On the other hand, Gericault was now living in the quarter called "La Nouvelle Athènes", the neighborhood of his friends, the painter Horace Vernet and the old Royalist Colonel Bro.[14] Denise Aimé-Azam gives a vivid image of the wealthy life at the Rue des Martyrs, and discusses another affair Gericault had with a woman whom she identified as Madame L'Allemand, the beautiful wife of a temporarily exiled Napoleonic general. In spite of the liaison with Alexandrine-Modeste, Gericault must have had other mistresses. A passionate correspondence between Gericault and a hitherto unknown woman, revealed for the first time in letters that surfaced at a Paris auction in 1985, gives us yet another important clue to this issue. Added to this are minor stories, such as the long-known letter to an anonymous female addressee; the correspondence again reveals a hot-tempered personality in accordance to other events.

Compared to other contemporary masters, Gericault created only a few drawings of the female nude, and no paintings at all. The identity of the models has aroused some discussion, albeit without proof. If we omit the nudes shown either in groups or as couples, we have a small number of beautiful drawings of single girls or women, which lead to other riddles about when and where they were drawn and whom they represent. One drawing with two figures, obviously showing the same young girl (Paris, Ecole des Beaux-Arts), may serve as an example: a copy of the so-called Calman sketch-book has a third figure in the form of a winged, dangerous-looking male. The connection is dubious: does the male observe the naked body of the girl, or is he just an added sketch, maybe in contrast between beauty and ugliness?

Similar mysteries occur in the portraits. Although they do not cover an important part of his œuvre, the few portraits are intimately related to the life of Gericault and nearly always represent the artist's close friends. We can deal here only in passing remarks about a very small group of female heads; the most interesting of which is in the Béziers Museum, and was identified by Clément as a model who lived on the Rue de la Lune and was called "La grosse Suzanne". Some ten years later the catalogue of the Walferdin sale in 1880 lists the same painting as Tête de femme. Sa Maîtresse. Lee Johnson, in 1981, tried to shed light on this puzzle, comparing the painting in Béziers with drawings of models in a previously undiscovered sketch-book by an unknown artist around 1820.[15]

Following Lorenz Eitner and Philippe Grunchec, I am inclined to identify the lady in the painting as Alexandrine-Modeste Caruel, the same sitter as in the beautiful drawing from the sketch-book by Gericault in the Kunsthaus, Zurich (fol. 47 recto), the likeness of which was mentioned by Johnson. If we look at the life and work of Gericault in general, nothing would be more outside the painter's character than to bring to life the features of a professional model in such a personal and tender interpretation. The Zurich sketch-book (fol. 17 recto) shows another female portrait with a more direct and realistic approach to the sitter; this drawing bears a striking likeness to the full-length portrait of a seated woman (in oil) representing Laure Bro, the wife of Colonel Bro.[16] The two portraits of Laure Bro give an excellent example of the distance within the range of respect and friendship, while the painting in Béziers and the related drawing in Zurich presumably representing Alexandrine-Modeste Caruel show, in my opinion, a spiritualized tenderness which is lacking in both portraits of Laure Bro.

The pictorial expression of tender feelings forms, after the birth of his illegitimate son in 1818, a leitmotiv in Gericault's work. In contrast to the subject of mother and child, the one of father and child appears several times in important compositions or sketches for projects, the best known of which is the father and child group in the Raft of the Medusa. With the exception of the Medusa, we have to look at drawings, where the subject matter appears for a first time in connection with the Wounded Cuirassier in 1814.[17] The next related drawing belongs to the Roman period—Roman Peasant with Child in his Arms.[18] After the Raft of the Medusa, Gericault also used the motif in the draft for the monumental composition Liberation of the Prisoners of the Spanish Inquisition;[19] other related drawings and a single sketch on the verso of the aforementioned draft show the importance of the small group for the artist himself.

Even if the use of autobiographical elements in art seems to be commonplace in the Romantic era, the case of Gericault constitutes an extreme position. The artist lived through his own experiences in such an intense and passionate way that we should always examine his work in view of a possible intermingling with his private life. Gericault's temperament comes through many elements of his œuvre and can be traced even in a highly polished composition such as the Raft of the Medusa. The interpretation of hitherto mysterious motifs[20] may benefit from further discoveries in Gericault's life, which, in more than one aspect, still forms a mystery in itself.

Zurich
February 1987

[1] Lorenz Eitner, *Géricault, His Life and Work,* Cornell University Press 1981, p. 11 and 36.

[2] Eitner, op. cit. 1985, p. 74.

[3] *Revue de l'Art,* 31, 1976, p. 73ss.

[4] Charles Clément, *Géricault, Etude biographique et critique,* 3rd ed., Paris 1879, p. 77/78.

[5] Eitner, op. cit. 1983, ills. 63-65, cf. also endnotes to chapter II, 110 and 111; Eitner, Géricault, exh. cat. 1971/72, Los Angeles, cat. nrs. 25; Philippe Grunchec, *Master Drawings by Gericault,* International Exhibition Foundation, Washington 1985, cat. nr. 26; "Judith decapitating Holophernes". Pencil. Bayonne, inv. 739 (a.i. 2060), 201: 128 mm.

[6] Clément's catalogue of the drawings is much less complete than the catalogue of the paintings; the author obviously considered many drawings as neglectable study material. In addition to the 197 (180 + 17 in the supplement) listed items Clément mentions quite often additional drawings and several groups of drawings in foot-notes without giving full particulars as he does in the catalogue.)

[7] Op. cit., 1983, p. 80.

[8] Eitner, op. cit. 1983, p. 104/105, ills. 88-90.

[9] Op. cit., 1983, p. 104, ill. 87.

[10] Op. cit., 1983, ill. 66; Grunchec, op. cit. 1985, cat. nr. 20 recto.

[11] Op. cit. 1983, p. 104/105, ills. 88-90; Grunchec, op. cit. 1985, cat. nr. 39.

[12] Cf. M. Tournex, "Particularités intimes sur la vie et l'œuvre de Géricault", *Bulletin de la Société de l'Histoire de l'Art Français,* 1912, p. 56ff.

[13] Cf. Pierre Courthion, *Géricault raconté par lui-même et par ses amis,* Vésenaz-Genève 1947, p. 232 with an argument about the truth of the incident, cf. also Eitner, op. cit. 1983, p. 214.

[14] Cf. Exh. cat. *La Nouvelle Athènes,* Musée Renan-Scheffer, Paris, 19 Juin-21 Octobre 1984; Denise Aimé-Azam, Mazeppa, Géricault et son Temps, Paris 1956, p. 147ss.

[15] Lee Johnson, " 'La grosse Suzanne' uncovered", *Burlington Magazine,* April 1981, p. 218ss.; Eitner, op. cit. 1983, p. 93, ill. 77; Philippe Grunchec, *Tout l'Œuvre peint de Gericault,* Paris 1978, cat. nr. 120.

[16] Grunchec, op. cit. 1978, cat. nr. 217.

[17] Grunchec, op. cit. 1985, cat. nr. 7 verso.

[18] Grunchec, op. cit. 1985, cat. nr. 35 verso and fig. 35a; the motif here is obviously inspired by a real scene.

[19] Eitner, op. cit. 1983, ill. 219; Grunchec, op. cit. 1985, cat. nr. 61 recto and verso.

[20] Cf. Grunchec, op. cit. 1985, cat. nr. 21 and the related remarks in the review of Lorenz Eitner, *Burlington Magazine,* January 1986, p. 55-59.

1. ***Couple Embracing***
pen and wash
12¼ × 8½ inches

2. ***Satyr and Nymph***
pen, black and red chalk, white wash
8⅜ × 5¼ inches

3. ***Judith Decapitating the Head of Holofernes*** (?)
chalk and pencil
8⅞ × 5⅜ inches

4. ***Bust of a Young Woman***
(Alexandrine-Modeste Caruel?)
from the Zurich Sketchbook (fol. 47 recto)
chalk and white gouache
10¾ × 8¼ inches

THE CATALOGUE
AND
ILLUSTRATIONS

THEODORE GERICAULT
Paintings

The following abbreviations are used in the catalogue listings:

Clément — Charles Clément, *Géricault: Etude Biographique et Critique,* Paris 1868.

Eitner, LA — Lorenz Eitner, *Géricault,* Los Angeles County Museum of Art, 1971; Detroit Institute of Arts, 1972; Philadelphia Museum of Arts, 1972.

Clément-Eitner — Reprint of 1879 edition of Clément, with introduction and supplement by Lorenz Eitner, Leonce Laget Editeur, 1973.

Grunchec — Philippe Grunchec, *Tout L'Œuvre Peint de Gericault,* Paris, 1978.

Eitner, Life — Lorenz Eitner, *Géricault: His Life and Work,* London, 1983.

1. *Two Horses in a Landscape* (c. 1808-9)
oil on canvas, 10¼ × 16 inches
Phillips Collection, Washington, D.C.
Grunchec A15, p. 130-31; Eitner, Life 2
Collections:
   Eugène Delacroix; M. Foinard; R. Goetz, Paris; Duc de Trévise, Paris; J. B. Neumann, New York, 1944.

2. *Episode de la Campagne d'Egypte (Mameluke Leading his Horse from Burning Barn),* (c. 1810-11)
oil on paper mounted to canvas, 6½ × 9¾ inches
Private Collection, New Jersey
Clément 19; Grunchec 138; Eitner, Life, fig. 11
Collections:
   A. Walferdin, Sale 12-16 April 1880, lot 127; Bazaine, Sale 23 January 1882, lot 25; Pierre Dubaut, Paris; Hans E. Bühler, Winterthur.
illustrated plate 1

3. *Le Sommeil des Apôtres* (c. 1808-12)
oil on panel, 30½ × 22½ inches
Clément-Eitner, p. 33, p. 299, no. 94, p. 321, no. 180; Grunchec no. 7.
Collections:
   Eugène Delacroix, Paris, Sale 17-19 February 1864, no. 228; Isambert, Paris, Sale 9 June 1867, no. 90; Boitelle, Paris, Sale 5 February 1912; André Dunoyer de Segonzac, Paris.
illustrated plate 3

4. *Portrait de Vieillard, d'après Rembrandt*
oil on canvas, 18 × 11¼ inches
Clément 176; Grunchec 6b
Collections:
   Charles Binder, 1892; P.-A. Chéramy; M. Boisgirard; Private Collection, Switzerland
illustrated plate 4

Note: Originally, the present painting was paired on a single canvas with a copy of Rembrandt's early *Self Portrait with a Gold Chain,* a work also preserved in the Louvre (Bredius 19). The copies were included in the post-mortem inventory of the contents of Gericault's studio, and they also figured in the artist's estate sale. By 1892, at the time of the Binder auction, the two copies had been separated. (See Grunchec 6a).

5. *Portrait of Simeon Bonnesoeur de la Bourginière* (c. 1811-12)
oil on canvas, 15⅞ × 12⅞ inches
Minneapolis Institute of Arts, The John R. Van Derlip and William Hood Dunwoody Funds
Clément 65; Eitner, LA no. 2
Collections:
   Henri Moulin, Mortain; Anonymous sale, Paris, Hôtel Drouot, 22 December 1922; Duc de Trévise, Paris; (B. Laurenceau, 1958)
illustrated plate 5

6. *Le Christ au Tombeau, d'après Titien*
oil on canvas, 17¾ × 23¼ inches
Musée Cantonal des Beaux-Arts, Lausanne, gift of Max Bangerter, 1966
Clément 165; Eitner, LA 6; Grunchec 28
Collections:
   Lehoux, 1897; L. Milich-Tambuid, Lugano.
illustrated plate 2

7. *Esquisse de l'Officier de Chasseurs à Cheval Chargeant* (c. 1812)
oil on canvas, 18⅛ × 15 inches
Clément 45; Eitner, LA 10; Grunchec A193
Collections:
   M. de la Rosière; Private Collection, Switzerland
illustrated plate 6

8. *Le Cuirassier Blessé* (c. 1813-14)
oil on canvas, 21¹¹/₁₆ × 18⅛ inches
The Brooklyn Museum, Anonymous Gift through the Macbeth Gallery
Clément 53; Eitner, LA 17; Grunchec 73
Collections:
   James-Nathaniel Rothschild, Paris; Martin Birnbaum, Paris; Private Collection, New York; (Macbeth Gallery 1943)
illustrated plate 7

9. *Le Cheval Blanc* (c. 1813-14)
oil on canvas, 23½ × 28¼ inches
Private Collection, Switzerland
Clément-Eitner p. 448; Grunchec 52E
Collections:
   Henri Rocheford (1903), Paris; Politiker; Otto Ackerman (1910-1915), Paris; Private Collection, Berlin
illustrated, plate 8

10. *Cheval Bai-clair et un autre Gris dans une Ecurie*
oil on paper mounted to canvas, 20 × 25½ inches
Private Collection, New Jersey
Grunchec A10
Collection:
   Baron Chasseriau; Colonel Nouvion
illustrated plate 9

11. *Trompette de Chasseur*
oil on canvas, 37¹³/₁₆ × 28⅜ inches
Sterling and Francine Clark Art Institute, Williamstown, MA
Clément 61bis; Eitner, LA 20; Grunchec 81; Eitner, Life, plate 14
Collections:
   Monjean; P. Crabbe, Brussels (1883); Baron Ury de Gunbourg; Defoer, Paris, Sale 22 May 1886, no. 20; G. Lutz, sale 26-27 May 1902, no. 68; Herman Schaus, New York; Elizabeth S. Clark; F. Ambrose Clark; R. S. Clark
illustrated plate 10

12. After Théodore Gericault
    Trompette de Chasseur
    oil on canvas, 14 × 10 inches
    Sterling and Francine Clark Art Institute, Williamstown, MA
    Grunchec 81A
    Note: This is a reduced copy of catalogue no. 11, kindly lent by the Clark Art Institute for comparison.

13. *Portrait d'Alfred Dedreux* (c. 1815-16)
    oil on canvas, 18 × 15 inches
    The Metropolitan Museum of Art, Alfred N. Punnett Endowment Fund, 1941
    Clément 14; Eitner, LA 23; Grunchec 95; Eitner, Life, plate 16
    Collections:
        Eugène Delacroix, Sale 17-19 February 164; R. Goetz, Sale 23-24 February 1922, no. 142; Duc de Trévise, Sale 19 March 1938, no. 30; Robert Lebel, Paris
    illustrated plate 11

14. *Mameluck de la Galerie d'Orléans*
    oil on canvas, 13 × 9½ inches
    Clément 58; Grunchec 161
    Collections:
        Duc d'Orléans (Incised monogram on stretcher bar); Walferdin, Sale 12-16 April 1880, no. 123; Antoine Vollon père; P.-A. Chéramy, sale 5-7 May 1908, no. 59; P.-A. Chéramy, Sale 14-16 April 1913, no. 386; Private Collection; Sotheby's 2 December 1970, no. 10; Private Collection
    illustrated plate 12

15. *Les Coqs et Poules et Cochon d'Inde*
    oil on paper mounted to canvas, 25¼ × 21 inches
    Clément 79; Clément-Eitner p. 452; Grunchec 82
    Collections:
        Lord Seymour, Sale 13-14 February 1860, no. 93; possibly Emile Blanc, Sale 7 April 1862, no. 26 (as "Coq et Poules"); Thiebault-Sisson, Sale 23 November 1907, no. 55; Dr. L. Voillemot; Cl. Offenstadt; Hans E. Bühler, Winterthur.
    Cover illustration.

16. *Lion* (c. 1816)
    oil on paper mounted to canvas, 10 × 15 inches
    Private Collection, Minneapolis
    Grunchec 145A
    Collections:
        Pierre Gaubert, Paris; Ambroselli, Paris
    illustrated plate 13

17. *Cinq Chevaux de Poil Différent* (c. 1816-17)
    oil on paper mounted to canvas, 9½ × 13 inches
    Bears initial at lower right: T.G.
    Private Collection
    Clément 91; Clément-Eitner 91, p. 452; Grunchec 99, plate XVIIIA
    Collections:
        A.M. His de la Salle; Comte Arnauld Doria, Paris; Jacques Dubourg, Paris
    illustrated plate 14
    note: See catalogue no. 34 for another version of this same subject.

18. *Le Radeau de la Méduse* (1818)
    brown ink on oil impregnated paper, 13 × 21¼ inches
    Eitner, *Géricault's Raft of the Medusa,* London, 1972, no. 23.
        Eitner, Life, pp. 173-174, note 104
    Collections:
        Courtin; Hans E. Bühler, Winterthur
    illustrated plate 15

19. *Portrait d'Homme* (Alexandre Corréard?) (1818)
    oil on canvas, 16⅛ × 13 inches
    bears initials: GLT 1818
    Eitner, *Géricault's Raft of the Medusa,* London, 1972, no. 105, Grunchec 168
    Collections:
        Leon Coignat, Paris; Mme. Payen; P.-A. Chéramy, Paris, Sale 5-7 May 1908, no. 67; Otto Ackerman; Hans E. Bühler, Winterthur
    illustrated plate 16

20. *L'Homme Nu*
    oil on canvas, 30 × 24½ inches
    Private Collection, Switzerland
    Clément 6; Grunchec 23
    Collections:
        A. M. Leconte, Paris; Private Collection, Paris
    illustrated plate 17
    Note: Clément lists this as an *académie* after the model Cadamour.

21. *Cheval Blanc Efraye (Après Stubbs)*
    oil on paper mounted to canvas, 11 × 13½ inches
    Private Collection, New York
    Clément 161
    Collections:
        A. M. Binder, Paris
    Note: Philippe Grunchec has suggested this as the left side of a composition taken from the famous Stubbs engraving, the other half pictured as Grunchec 194B.

22. *Scène de la Guerre de l'Indépendance Grecque* (c. 1818-20)
    oil on canvas, 15 × 18¼ inches
    Virginia Museum of Fine Arts, Richmond, The Williams Fund, 1959.
    Clément 149; Eitner, LA 114; Grunchec 131, pl. XXIV; Eitner, Life, fig. 179.
    Collections:
        Leconte; Bischoffsheim; P.-A. Chéramy, Paris, Sale 6-7 May 1908 no. 58; Lierens, Brussels, Sale 22-23 December 1931, no. 38; Pierre Dubaut, Paris; G. Renand, Paris; Durlacher Bros., New York
    illustrated plate 18

23. *Jockey Montant un Cheval de Course* (1820-22)
    oil on canvas, 14½ × 18¼ inches
    Virginia Museum of Fine Arts, Richmond, Gift of Mr. and Mrs. Paul Mellon
    Clément 138 (?); Clément-Eitner, no. 138, p. 456; Grunchec 199A
    Collections:
        Coolidge, Topsfield, MA; (Knoedler, New York 1960); Mr. and Mrs. Paul Mellon
    illustrated plate 19

24. *Deux Chevaux de Ferme à la Porte* (c. 1823)
    oil on canvas, 9¹/₁₆ × 12⅞ inches
    Private Collection
    Grunchec 234
    Collections:
        Hans E. Bühler, Winterthur
    illustrated, plate 20

25. *La Tempête* (c. 1822-23)
    oil on paper mounted to canvas, 13⅜ × 20¾ inches
    Yale University Art Gallery, New Haven, Stephen Carlton Clark Fund
    Eitner, LA, 118; Grunchec A138
    Collections:
        Drs. F. and P. Nathan, Zurich
    illustrated plate 21

26. *Marine* (c. 1822-23)
oil on canvas, 18½ × 22¹/₁₆ inches
Clément 17; Eitner, LA, 115; Grunchec 222, plate LIII
Collections:
　Paul Flandrin, Paris; M. Moureaux; Alfred Stevens; Marmontel, Sale 28-29 March 1898, no. 96; O. Ackermann; Private Collection, Switzerland.
illustrated frontice piece

ADDENDUM

Tête de Supplice
oil on paper mounted to panel, 16⅛ × 14¹⁵/₁₆ inches
Eitner, LA, no. 90; Grunchec 175, illus. XXXVIII; Eitner, Life fig. 170, illus. p. 181, ref pp. 183-4
Collections:
　A. Boulard; Duc de Trévise; P. Dubaut, Paris; Private Collection

WATERCOLORS, DRAWINGS, PRINTS AND SCULPTURE

27. *Italian Buildings*
brown ink and wash on paper, 5¼ × 4¼ inches

Reclining Classical Figure
brown ink and wash on paper, 3 × 4½ inches
Collections:
　Marquis Philippe de Chennevières, Paris, (Lugt no. 2072); Dr. A. Politzer, Vienna, (Lugt no. 2741).
illustrated plate 23

28. *Warrior Figure Group* (c. 1813-14)
(After Girolamo Romano's *Battle of Constantine*)
pencil on paper highlighted with gall ink, 6¾ × 5¼ inches
Private Collection
Collections:
　M. Normand, Paris; Galerie Bayser, Paris; André Salomon, Paris, Estate of André Salomon, Paris; Salander-O'Reilly Galleries, Inc., New York
illustrated plate 22

29. *Study of a Nude Man Holding a Rearing Horse*
pen and ink on paper, 9⅞ × 7½ inches
Nelson-Atkins Museum of Art, Kansas City, MO, The Nelson Fund
Eitner, LA 45
Collections:
　Michel-Levy (Sale 1919); Duc de Trévise (Sale 1938)
illustrated plate 24

30. *Empereur Casqué Retenant un Homme Fuyant* (c. 1817)
pen and brown ink over traces of pencil, 4¼ × 3½ inches
Collections:
　Eric Carlson, New York; Colnaghi USA, Ltd., New York; Private Collection
illustrated plate 34
Note: Dr. Lorenz Eitner has dated this work 1817 and compared it with two similar drawings of the same figures in the Musée Bonnat, Bayonne.

31. *The French Farrier*
pen and brown ink, some point of brush, and pencil on paper, 8¼ × 5⁵/₁₆ inches
Private Collection, New York
Collections:
　David Carritt, London
illustrated plate 31

32. *Fall of the Rebel Angels (After Rubens)*
pencil on paper, 8¹/₁₆ × 9¹/₁₆ inches
Stanford Art Museum, Stanford, CA
Eitner, LA, no. 76
Collections:
　E. Deveria, Paris

33. *Return of Tobias* (c. 1817-18)
gouache on paper, 8¼ × 7⅛ inches
Private Collection, Switzerland
Collections:
　Coutau-Huguet, 16-17 December 1889, no. 174; Vente Levevre, 1895.
illustrated plate 26

34. *Groom Holding Four Horses*
pencil on paper, 7⅝ × 9³/₁₆ inches
Private Collection, New York
Collections:
　Pierre Dubaut, Paris; Walter Goetz, Paris
illustrated plate 25
Note: see catalogue no. 17, plate 14 for another version of this subject.

35. *Six Heads* (Studies for the *Raft of the Medusa*) (1818)
black chalk, 9¾ × 15½ inches
Metropolitan Museum of Art, Bequest of Walter C. Baker
Collections:
　Jean-François Gigoux, Paris, Sale 20-23 March 1822, no. 593 (with another drawing *Un Homme Assis, Vu de Dos*); Emmanuel-Charles Benezit(?); Wildenstein, New York; Walter C. Baker, New York
illustrated plate 27

36. *Two Male Nudes* (Studies for the *Raft of the Medusa*) (1818)
pencil on paper, 9¹/₁₆ × 13½ inches
The Art Museum, Princeton University, Princeton, NJ, Museum Purchase
illustrated plate 28

37. *Le Radeau de la Méduse* (ca. 1820)
watercolor on paper, 4¼ × 6½ inches
Jan Krugier, Geneva
Clément 139B; Eitner, Lorenz, *Géricault's Raft of the Medusa*, London 1972, p. 152, no. 28
Collections:
　A. Corréard, Paris; M. Leclère Fils, Paris; M. Rouher, Paris (Prime Minister under Napoléon III); Marquise Samuel Velles de la Valette (daughter of M. Rouher); Private Collection, France, by descent.
Note: This watercolor was made by Gericault for the fourth edition of Corréard's and Savigny's "Méduse", published 1821. This is the second in the series for that edition.

38. *Des Officiers Anglais Visitant Corréard et les Rescapés après leur Sauvetage* (c. 1820)
watercolor on paper, 4¼ × 6½ inches
Jan Krugier, Geneva
Clément 139D; Eitner, Lorenz, *Géricault's Raft of the Medusa*, London 1972, p. 173, no. 112
Collections:
　IBID.
Note: see preceeding.

39. *Le Ministre du Roi Zaide Traçant la Carte de l'Europe* (c. 1820)
watercolor on paper, 4¼ × 6½ inches
Jan Krugier, Geneva
Clément 139C; Eitner, Lorenz, *Géricault's Raft of the Medusa*, London, 1972, p. 173, no. 111
Collections:
　ref. no. 37
Note: ref. no. 37

40. *Chevaux Harnachés* (recto)
Cheval (verso)
pencil on paper, 6⅞ X 11 inches
Collections:
M. S. Romao (collection stamp); Hans E. Bühler, Winterthur
illustrated plate 29 (recto); plate 30 (verso)
Note: Although Gericault's interest in horses as subject matter begins early in his career, this drawing appears to relate most directly to work done in London in 1820 and 1821, including the *Entrance to the Adelphi Wharf, from La Serie Anglaise* (lithograph, 1821) and the watercolors *Groom with Horse* (1820-21) in the Louvre and *Groom with Two Horses* in the Fogg Art Museum.

41. *Je Rêve d'elle au Bruit des Flots* (c. 1820)
watercolor, wash and crayon on paper, 3¼ X 4⅜ inches
Mrs. Marie-Anne Krugier, Geneva

Grunchec, referred to under no. 7
Collections:
Pierre Dubaut, Paris (Lugt supplement, 2103b); André Salomon, Paris

Note: This is a study for a lithograph published in 1822 illustrating the song "Amédée de Beauplan". Dr. Paul Joannides states in an article "Towards the dating of Géricault's Lithographs" (Burlington Magazine, vol. CXV, no. 847, October 1973, pp. 666-671) that this lithograph was based on an Eighteenth century story, Nadir, after A. Gautier de Mont-dorge, re-issued in September 1922. The Byronic character in this watercolor represents Alp, the renegade of the seige of Corinth meditating on the sea shore.

42. *Mazeppa*
gouache, watercolor on paper, 7¼ X 8¼ inches
Private Collection, Switzerland
Collections:
Calmann, London
illustrated plate 32

43. *Satyr and Nymph*
posthumous bronze cast height 11¹/₁₆ inches
The Art Museum, Princeton University, Princeton, NJ, Gift of Edward W. Pell
illustrated plate 33

44. *Chariot Chargé de Soldats Blessés* (1818)
lithograph, Delteil II ii/ii

45. *Lara Blessé*
lithograph, Delteil 45, iii/iv

46. *La Jumet et son Poulain* (1822)
lithograph, Delteil 46, iii/v

47. *Mazeppa* (1823)
lithograph, Delteil 94, iii/iii (with Eugene Lami)
(This is an undescribed state between Delteil's second and third states).

1. **Episode de la Campagne d'Egypte** (c. 1810-11)
oil on paper mounted to canvas, 6½ × 9¾ inches
Private Collection, New Jersey
Catalogue no. 2

2. **Le Christ au Tombeau, d'après Titien**
oil on canvas, 17¾ × 23¼ inches
Musée Cantonal des Beaux-Arts, Lausanne, Gift of Max Bangerter
Catalogue no. 6

3. **Le Sommeil des Apôtres** (c. 1808-12)
oil on panel, 30½ X 22¼ inches
Catalogue no. 3

4. **Portrait de Vieillard, d'après Rembrandt**
oil on canvas, 18 X 11¼ inches
Catalogue no. 4

5. ***Portrait of Simeon Bonnesoeur de la Borginière*** (c. 1811-12)
oil on canvas, 15⅞ × 12⅞ inches
Minneapolis Institute of Arts, John R. Van Derlip and
William Hood Dunwoody Funds
Catalogue no. 5

6. ***Esquisse de l'Officier de Chasseurs à Cheval Chargeant*** (c. 1812)
oil on canvas, 18⅛ × 15 inches
Catalogue no. 7

7. *Le Cuirassier Blessé* (c. 1813-14)
oil on canvas, 21 $^{11}/_{16}$ X 18⅛ inches
The Brooklyn Museum, Anonymous Gift through the Macbeth Gallery
Catalogue no. 8

8. **Le Cheval Blanc** (c. 1813-14)
oil on canvas, 23½ × 28¼ inches
Private Collection, Switzerland
Catalogue no. 9

9. **Cheval Bai-clair et un autre Gris dans une Ecurie**
oil on paper mounted to canvas, 20 × 25½ inches
Private Collection, New Jersey
Catalogue no. 10

10. **Trompette de Chasseur**
oil on canvas, 37¹³/₁₆ × 28⅜ inches
Sterling and Francine Clark Art Institute, Williamstown
Catalogue no. 11

11. ***Portrait d'Alfred Dedreux*** (c. 1815-16)
oil on canvas, 18 × 15 inches
The Metropolitan Museum of Art,
The Alfred N. Punnett Endowment Fund
Catalogue no. 13

12. **Mameluck de la Galerie d'Orléans**
oil on canvas, 18 × 15 inches
Catalogue no. 14

13. **Lion** (c. 1816)
oil on paper mounted to canvas, 10 × 15 inches
Private Collection, Minneapolis
Catalogue no. 16

14. **Cinq Chevaux de Poil Différent** (c. 1816-17)
oil on paper mounted to canvas, 9½ × 13 inches
Private Collection
Catalogue no. 17

15. ***Le Radeau de la Méduse*** (1818)
brown ink on oil impregnated paper
13 × 12¼ inches
Catalogue no. 18

16. ***Portrait d'Homme*** (Alexandre Corréard?) (1818)
oil on canvas, 16⅛ × 13 inches
Catalogue no. 19

17. **_L'Homme Nu_**
oil on canvas, 30 × 24¼ inches
Private Collection, Switzerland
Catalogue no. 20

18. *Scène de la Guerre de l'Indépendance Grecque* (c. 1818-20)
oil on canvas, 15 × 18¼ inches
Virginia Museum of Fine Arts, The Williams Fund
Catalogue no. 22

19. *Jockey Montant un Cheval de Course* (1820-22)
oil on canvas, 14½ × 18¼ inches
Virginia Museum of Fine Arts, Gift of Mr. and Mrs. Paul Mellon
Catalogue no. 23

20. **_Deux Chevaux de Ferme à la Porte_** (c. 1832)
oil on canvas, 9¹/₁₆ × 12⅞ inches
Private Collection
Catalogue no. 24

21. **_La Tempête_** (c. 1822-23)
oil on paper mounted to canvas, 13⅜ × 20¾ inches
Yale University Art Gallery, Stephen Carlton Clark Fund
Catalogue no. 25

22. ***Warrior Figure Group*** (c. 1813-14)
(After Girolamo Romano's *Battle of Constantine*)
pencil on paper highlighted with gall ink,
6¾ × 5¼ inches
Private Collection
Catalogue no. 28

23. *Italian Buildings*
brown ink and wash on paper,
5¼ × 4¼ inches

Reclining Classical Figure
brown ink and wash on paper,
3 × 4½ inches
Catalogue no. 27

24. ***Study of a Nude Man Holding a Rearing Horse***
pen and ink on paper, 9⅞ X 7½ inches
Nelson-Atkins Museum of Art, The Nelson Fund
Catalogue no. 29

25. ***Groom Holding Four Horses***
pencil on paper, 7⅝ × 9³/₁₆ inches
Private Collection, New York
Catalogue no. 34

26. **Return of Tobias** (c. 1817-18)
gouache on paper, 8¼ × 7⅛ inches
Private Collection, Switzerland
Catalogue no. 33

27. **Six Heads** (Study for the *Raft of the Medusa*) (1818)
black chalk on paper, 9¾ × 15½ inches
Metropolitan Museum of Art, Bequest of Walter C. Baker
Catalogue no. 35

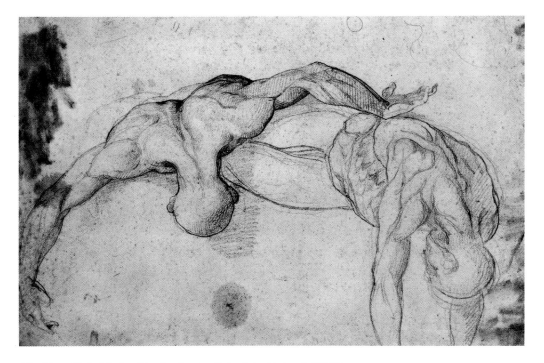

28. **Two Male Nudes** (Studies for the *Raft of the Medusa*) (1818)
Pencil on paper, 9¹/₁₆ × 13½ inches
The Art Museum, Princeton University, Museum Purchase
Catalogue no. 36

29. **Chevaux Harnachés** (recto)
pencil on paper, 6⅞ × 11 inches
Catalogue no. 40

30. **Cheval** (verso)
pencil on paper, 6⅞ × 11 inches
Catalogue no. 40

31. **The French Farrier**
pen and brown ink, some point of brush and pencil on paper,
8¼ × 5⁵/₁₆ inches
Private Collection, New York
Catalogue no. 31

32. *Mazeppa*
gouache, watercolor on paper, 7¼ × 8¼ inches
Private Collections, Switzerland
Catalogue no. 42

33. **Satyr and Nymph**
postumous bronze cast, height 11¹/₁₆ inches
The Art Museum, Princeton University. Gift of Edward W. Pell
Catalogue no. 43

34. **Empereur Casqué Retenant un Homme Fuyant** (c. 1817)
pen and brown ink over traces of pencil, 4¼ × 3½ inches
Catalogue no. 30

BCK GRAPHIC ARTS SA
29, rue de la Synagogue
Geneva
PRINTED IN SWITZERLAND